Waterfall

Classical Romantic Poetry and Prose

Patrick Shortall

MMXV

First published in 2015 by Patrick Shortall
This second edition published in 2016

Edited by Sadhbh Ní Bhroin
Layout design by Dáithí O Broin
Set in Perpetua 12 and 14 point
Publishing consultancy by www.carrowmore.ie

Conditions of Sale

Shortall, Patrick
Waterfall, Classical Romantic Poetry and Prose, MMXV
ISBN 978-0-9934171-0-8

– Appreciation –

I offer "My Greatest Appreciation" with
"Profound – Poetic – Pleasure"
to the following institutions:

Trinity College Dublin, Ireland

National Museum of Ireland

National Library of Ireland

for their Loyalty and Patronage

Every Tiny –
Bubble –
Beatifying –
Nature's – Creation –

Contents

"WATERFALL"

I

Graciously Lies from Rocks –
To The Skies –
Sweet – Beautiful A "Waterfall" –
Perfumed Petals Of Love –
Showering Low From Above –
Spraying Scents On –
All Who Call –

II

Gushing – Rushing – Flushing – Flowing –
Rolling – Rocking – Rowing –
Scribbling The Rocks –
Looping The Ferns –
Where Butterflies Ensemble In Flocks –

III

Glory Gracefully Lies On Rocks –
To The Skies –
Sweet – Beautiful – A "Waterfall"
Eternally – There –
Tiny – Bubbles – To Share –
Beatifying – All Who Call –

A ROSE IN MY HEART

I

I Feel A Rose Growing
In My Heart –
A "Peach Pink Rose"
My Pulse – The Wind –
Willowing – Wavering – Wandering
Pondering – Bending –
"Awakening Our Teens" –

II

Youth And Age – The Bridge –
Of Time –
Spanning The "CROSSOVER"
Of Yester – Years And Now

III

"Youth The Master –
Of Age" –
"SPENT TIME" –

IV

I Feel A Rose Growing
In My Heart –
A "Peach Pink Rose"
My Pulse – The Breathing Breeze
Humming –
A Pendulum – Ticking –
Winding –

MOONLOVE

There is no love in this Moonlight
Nor music in the air
Or sharing hearts or holding hands
Not dreaming lovers dare

No flesh of youth of frisking feel
When touching lips become unreal
The stars that dance a jigging reel
This night no presence share

No lyrics in the quavered night
Or love shadows in candlelite
Lonely, lonely lips ice cold bite
Nakedly but there

There is no love in this Moonlight
But sadness in the air
No warmth of blood in veins of flesh
Caressing bodies bare

Cold alone, care for this night
Nothing else but breathe of sight
Casts on all it's blossomed blight
Lingers love beware

No moonlove in this Moonlite
Love has lost eternal right
When comes day but after night
Dead souls with lovers share

AUTUMN

Fol'um ~ Solum – Leaf ~ Ground

Tints of August colours, sweep creep the Aurum sky
Peach redden cloud falls its mist, to ground where damp it lies
Shaken trees of naked wind, birds twiggen nest rest share
Fluttered flight of branches height, softly sway the air

Moon beams break from deepened light, Autumn is but there
Wakens Winter of cold its bed, nature now must share
Blustering breeze its wind with ease, meets of old a friend
Blowing blowing blowing, for Summer is but end

Cold ice chills on granite sills, of Moonlight white grey glisten
Bare of sound of birds around, for now alas we listen
Acorns grieve its fruit oak leave, to grass pale brown they lay
Bright long nights of sunshine bright, fade afar away

Shades shadowed sketch on pavement left, lay rest dry fol'um
Spent life now over trod foot by rover, quell embeds the solum
Chestnuts fall when dark nights call, gust blown along the way
Rolling rolling rolling to nowhere, but astray

Flaunting Flakes sail down to lakes, its rippled water frozen
'Twas but yester time, new born duckling's bosom
Glints of Autumn sapphire, trawl the twilight tide
Nature bares with Winter; till Season changes stride

PLOUGH & STARS

I Heard A Darling Little Poem
Sent with Magic, The World to Roam
It knew a String, knew a Balloon
Sailed to the Sky in Afternoon

Paid a visit to Planet Mars
Then jumped upon the Plough and Stars
It Wrote its way to Jupiter
Then it ended — no Furtherer

Then left one Verse of lines Behind
To tell the Galaxy of Mankind
Blowing Home To Earth for Free
Without That Verse Of Poetry

for Isaac

15

BROKEN SILENCE

There is a NOISE that breaks
The SILENCE —
Pounding in my BRAIN —
Like BEATING SOUND a thousand DRUMS
Speeding fast a TRAIN —

And when that THUNDER rattles me
An EARTHQUAKE great I HEAR —
ROARING, ROCKING, ROARING
Bursts, RUMBLING in my Ear —

I FEEL the noise THUMP in my HEART
Torments my inward SOUL —
The NOISE had – it a COLOUR
Would be as BLACK as COAL —

And when the NOISE has passed AWAY
Its ECHOES far long GONE —
I hear a NOISE that breaks
The SILENCE —
Haranguing — Banging — ON —

JOYUS SEA

Waves break brilliant on the Sea
Watch I them jump and dance the spr'y
Foam it smiles of Noon delite
As the Sky, is smirking brite

Gulls are flapping Flock the Rocks
Black and white in feathered smocks
Fish are swimming through the reeds
Tiny making, bubbling beeds

Moonward tide lands, wets the sands
Never idle, never stands
To the West sinks the Sun
Tranquil sleepy, nite's begun

Homeward Crawl I Pleasure Be
Oft' Would I Like To See that Sea

SUMMER

I feel the Sound of murmuring Summer
Blossoms Suck, the warming air
Flowers are opening all their petals
Scents of Sweet for LIFE to share

I watch the lambs Fleece Ruffle Fur
Bleating fleeting, a new born purr
Hares make-chase, 'round frisk race
Glorious be, buds fragrance grace

I hear the Bird's broods ever sing
Lands to my ear, full warble ring
Leaves FLIRT– DANCE upon the trees
Flurrying joyfully amongst slite breeze

I see a Sky blue high a Sun
Shining down, till dusk it come
I feel I hear watch I, then see
A passionate fling Summer BE

WILDE
In Memoriam

In Reading Gaol there is no bail
Nor freedom of any chance
Just the smell, of a living hell
And a warder there to glance
With no one there no joy to share
Mad spirits come to prance
On a poor old soul, locked in a hole
And dies in Paris, France

From bleak cell walls, where madness falls
And drips to a cell floor
A playwright who was once so great
Is locked behind a door
His mind is chained, with hands refrained
Not writing anymore
A brain is now a prisoner
Torturous thoughts of what's in store

In Reading Gaol there is no bail
Nor freedom of any chance
You do your time whatever your crime
Appeals get but a glance
For C.3.3. it's sad to see
A man so great destroyed
Alas! your fate cannot be changed
Your genial works enjoyed

C.3.3.
OSCAR WILDE'S Prison Number
Block C, Floor 3, Cell 3.

23

ROSES

Awake Me From My Dreaming Sleep
Take Me To Where, Roses Creep
Long the meadowed path its way
Where glitters golden, suckles day

Be I there when NOON is high
Fondling Clouds blueth sky
Above the meadow may I see
Falls nature's blooms on harmony

Nest my dreams amongst thy flowers
Whilst a cuckoo! songs the hours
See I Roses, dance 'round love-tease
As RAINBOW lips, smile kiss, brite breeze

Fly my thoughts unto young Trees
Resting, cuddled in their Leaves
Slipping softly shall I Grace
Wander I, Sun's gleaming Place

Wake I The Nites Dreaming Sleep
Bring Me To Where, Roses Creep

PHANTOM

I hear a VOICE cry calling me
A VOICE I do not know —
Wakening, SHAKING —
When sleep is right
In darkening, glimmering
GLOW —

Who is this PHANTOM?
Stalk — HAWKS the NITE
When rests all SOULS —
SLEEPING!
Quiet —

I hear a VOICE, cry calling me
Cry calling me —
HOME —

Is it a howling GHOST of DEATH?
Interred deep HUNT haunts —
The EARTH —

Hear I a VOICE, cry calling me
Cry calling me — HOME —

It is the NITE —
VILLAIN be quiet!!!

RAINDROPS

COME RAIN COMETH!
Thy bloomy flowers make sigh!
Fall thee make the pastures new
Sky rivers downward cry!

—

Curse not the drops that wets the eye
Befalls the rain grey dullen sky
For if the rain, it cometh not
All nature's glory 'twill ruin of rot!

—

Whenas a thunder cloud doth burst
Bequeaths to Earth
Quench; quells its thirst
Flagging leaves of dripping wet
Thereon the trees, where rain has set

—

Glisten drops on petals young
Stay oh stay till lands the sun
Soaken, sweeten fragrance share
Flutter moists amongst thy air

—

If a foe of rain thou be!
Sweet smell the air its jollity
See I the rain it pleaseth me
A friend of all it ought to be!

—

Oft' when I hear the rain lash down
Splashing, lashing on the ground
Dance I in puddles with romancing
FLASH BACKS, MY YOUTH IN FANTASTY

SUNSET ON HISTORY

A moment of History falls upon us
Full tidal opportunity has begun
Offer we, a hand, which be friendly
For the sake, of Life, Daughter and Son

Born, Sunrise a new beginning
Honour we, equal land each one
May the soil, toil tilled flourish fruitful
Auld time, when its race be run

New Moon, glows over our mountains
While our rivers, flow ripples of love
Looms peace all 'round our valleys
Stars great, brite the nite above

Twilight of Noon, lands upon us
Eve's leafy lite, is nigh done
Harvest we, our hopes fate's fortune
Till the Sunset on History be Shone

SO — BE — IT

My Soul Has Nested —
In A Cradle Of Rest —
Of Memories — Gone By —

Sleeping With My Youth —
Leaving — Times Journey
Landing Upon Me —
Age —

A — Mirror of —
Reflected Past —
Suckling My Thoughts —
A Honeypot —
Meditating — My Life

SO — BE — IT

RINGSEND ROSY

Over Ringsend Sky, where Seagulls fly
When PEACE with SLEEP have met
All is left of the trawling night
Is a FISH that's caught in a net

In the MARITIME MORN, day is born
And the mist befriends Sunrise
There I walk with Ringsend Rosy
With a glint of love in her eyes

There we skip and hop, like seas that chop
Long by Sandymount Strand
Wander there a friend so rare
Love time, we both hold hands

In the fading day and the Sun has gone away
Calm with peace settles down
Then I sit with Rosy, SWEETHEART COSY
Down in Ringsend, Dublin Town

SOMETIME

Sometimes in LIFE LIFE is not fair
Answers we ask are simply not there
We think and try to work it all out
A mystery of fate an act brought about

Sometimes in LIFE we do what is best
Even our limit is pushed to its test
Deep in our heart we SEEK trying to find
Asking ourselves why life's being unkind

Sometimes in LIFE our dreams fall apart
Leaving us lost alone in the dark
At times we LAUGH at times we cry
Sometime in LIFE we all have to try
Never forgotten, are friends who standby

THE BEGGARMAN

"Are ye there? are ye there?"
Came the beggar mans call!
"Or are ye asleep in your bed?"
Then he thought to himself
In the darken night
Maybe! They're just only dead!

"I'll try for again a second time"
With his voice he left a roar!
"Sur' if I don't get an answer
For the last time
I'll try once more!"

He left a shout! heard miles about!
Fled carried! blew over the roofs
When all of a sudden
Heard what he thought
Inside the house a few moves!!

But a twig on the sill, Had broken the still
Fell twitch! on the beggar man's nose
He cursed to himself
As he walked from the house
On The Grass In The Cold To Repose!!!

Parody

BLOOMSDAY

You left to me of Joycean school
Learned knowledge upon a scroll
A language which was far and wide
A Ulysses beyond the tide
Deep of meaning if understood
Flows flowering verbal in its bud

But I shall quake and quiver deeply
Into your brain discover meekly
An understanding of what you wrote
You cryptic verbal, literary poet

If I fail in simplistic miss
Your verbal tongue tied English myth
Far far above the world removed
Your prodigal Ulysses beloved
A brain a mind which understands
The genius working of your hand

Oh! trip for which you took us dearly
Crawling home tiresome weary
Others they say you're of great note
I write to you THIS literary note
For what you have, Joyce, left behind
A cryptic manuscript to all mankind

VOYAGE OF SORROWS - TITANIC

I

Set Sail Great Ship, Voyage Sorrow's Trip
Beyond And Far Away
Wan Waters Deep, Will Mystery Reap
Not See You Land Or Quay

Set Sail Great Ship, Voyage Virgin Sail
Of iron cast well lade
Leave now this day, far away
Hail tale, sink sea forbade

Set Sail Oh Ship, Voyage Maiden Trip
Far yonder on sea wave
Lurks danger there, care, beware!
If ne'er rest be thy grave

Wild Beastly Be, The Sea Thou See
Sad souls of sailors lost
Low foreign waves in water caves
Sea farers found to cost

This Ship Be Dammed Iceberg Rammed
Once rivets fasten hold
Burst, but gush, woe Floes of Flush
Nay save by brave this cold

This Ship Hours Two, Would Be Askew
Cold furnace fires fed quench
Cold ice of water on her
Black oil her Cockles Drench

Black Founder Nite, Casks Water Tight
Flout face at dreams so rare
Near nigh stroke twelve
Life slip would delve
Wake sleep dread share nitemare

Harsh Hellish Hole, Rocks Demon Roll
Mad mercy made sick pain
The palm of fate, cruel hand hard hate
Know nought of tide refrain

From Star Its' Side, Rock Rip Long Wide
Of death knell sound it made
Sink water deep of fathoms steep
Drown iron cage, fast fade

II

Flash Floods Of Slush, Came Peril Purge Rush
Haunt hold, bow stern through deck
Demon water, twisted iron
Curse carnage, wanton's wreck

Hell Captured Night, Wet Torrents Rife
Repel nor see its rage
Flew anger flight, full brim drab nite
Whelm water's prison cage

This Sea Of Hell, Bloat Body Swell
Float dead, rigor mortis cold
Struck tragedy unthinkable
Hath unsinkable, unfold

Gaunt haunt screams sound
Doomed souls who drowned
Eery echo daunts its air
Stole young from old, thief death of cold
Deep pain bore born despair

Of scarlet purple, ghast gaunt of white
This sea its prey did swallow
Death masks float faces, drift its waves
Ear eerie sounds howl hollow

Suck sucklin' sea full lifeless be
Stole life in slept of night
Where spirits roam, soul's hell home
Bright after darken light

Dare Devil be, mid Skeleton Sea
The living and the dea
Wrath fury, fought, ire anger
Sink not this ship, swore said

Droop Davits Dropped held wood by prop
Fell fear with tilt each sway
Safe sacred saved, the cauldron braved
Yet live another day

Rests iron decay, 'neath lead clouds lay
Casts Cold its Cloak of black
Held fast those swam in water
Clung saved upon the Rack

45

III

Souls aye afar a many
Boats yea bar a few
Drown behind, nite Blacken Blind
Its Captain and his crew

Sad sailing Tomb, death water gloom
Full fathoms rest would lay
Murk mud of silt, its tiller tilt
Nay 'gain see life of day

Naught 'twas in the ganger's plan
To rest where doth it lay
Set Sail no more, Set Sail no more
Make stream another day

Of a Captain's beard, Worn Worse face feared
Life, family, friends loyal crew
Save some but seven hundred
Peril Perish the rest he knew

Struck Stricken deck, broke wretched wreck
Saw grim the Captain's eye
Cast Curse upon this water
Nigh time for him to die

Sleep now they rest, 'low wetten crest
Yonder of the bay
Nay Dream Again, Nay Seen Again
Once more another day

Life hath bedded death that nite
As Water Wades Wet tide
Had taken ship, once was proud
Crushed iceberg all its pride

Great ocean sorrow, by Dawn of Morrow
Flow death with tidal rage
Bathe blood froze flesh, had death full met
Froth forth of iron cage

Moonless Briteless Was The Nite
Waters dead of ripples quiet
Nor was there lapping :
Froth or foam, eyes for to peel
Where icebergs roam

There was but a stilly nite
No water wrinkled Moon
A Harvest Hell!
Of Bloody Swell!
Alas!
Would come too soon

A shadowed shade
Black:
Cloaks the waves
Dark be:
Its mask of death
Drowned dark deep
Mud, silten heap
Rest souls,
In phantom graves

When the Moon, nite's Labour Done
Salt mist began to Rise
Scorn Scowl thereon, dread deed fate foul
The morn its wanion eyes

Deep Dark Despair, filled Bleak Black air
As the Sun of Mourn Rose Strong
Gloat, deep, drub, pound, voice dead of sound
Hope lost of life was gone

Dread High Drown Toll, Fifteen Hundred Souls
Lost Seaward On That Day
Sad Ship Of Dreams
Sank Ship Of Dreams
Fathoms Deep From Land Or Bay

FELLOWS

We ought to speak on their behalf
Those who cannot speak themselves
Let them know they're not forgotten
Like the dust that's left on shelves

Friends are our precious ones
Left to us in trust and care
Surely there is too much and plenty
Rich and poor the world to share

We ought to help those in need
Those in sorrow suffering pain
Not thinking of our selfish greed
Let honour and mercy be our gain

We ought not to think but of ourselves
Rather helping those who can't themselves

GENTLE CHILD

Oh ! gentle child one marvel morn
Great flowering birth for us was born
An Angel simple blossoming sweet
A tiny tot this world to greet

A budding hope, a light of ray
For us to love and mind each day
To bless and cherish and hold love tight
Throughout the hours of dark and bright

Oh ! gentle child shall beauty grow
Showering forth with loving glow
You were with us a treasure while
Bright as stars your simple smile

Until such time we meet again
THIS POEM FOR YOU ENDS AMEN.

JACK THE MOUSE

I am a friendly happy Mouse
Jack! I reside, inside your House
NO CHANCE! You'll catch ME
With Cheese in Trap!
A spring in wood my neck to Snap!!!

A hole I have where not you know
Freely I can come and go
On crumbs you waste I like to Feed!
Simply fills, my belly's Need!!!

I am your guest pay I no rent
Stay will I, till I be spent
And when that day has come and Gone!
My family many will still hang On !!!

For love I dearly, MY LITTLE HOUSE

Forever yours,
Jack!
The Mouse!!!

for Leah

LIFFEY BROWN

"Why is the Liffey always Brown?"
Asked strange a Lady, with fore' of frown
Quicken thought did I say
"From Arthur Guinness up the way"

"Really is it !" then she said !
"Of course" says I, "there's its bed
See The Pipes Off Quay Walls Flow
Over there the Stout it goes"

Why is the Liffey always brown?
Beckoning eyes we both look down
Frothy waters that's Guinness foam
"Sur'"says I "it's Dublin's home"

Is the Liffey always brown?
Think I with Wonder, in this my Town
"Wait" says she, "look! Arthur spouting"
Strange Lady Smiling, No Longer Doubting

LEFT I A FLOWER

Left I A Flower Strewn
On a grave —
In deep my darkest Day
Then sadly with a Tear
On Cheek
Sad simply walked Away

An Orchid pretty Just —
But one —
My tear had fallen On
My love had she —
Departed —
To a place unknown beyond

When I Returned
Orchids many
Put me to Blush and Shame
Growing in the Garden
Thousands —
Proud Shrouding In Her Name

LULLABY LAKE

Breast, on a stump of Tree I sat
Flowed to me Fish who swam the wet
Of Worms, on hooks, freeze wriggle cold
The fish to me a tale it told

Sprang from a Lake, flowers grew
Milk nectar stains, were Bees on shoe
Out of its water, a Fox ! a sprout !
On its back, brown dancing Trout !

Burst of a cloud, a Rabbit roar !
Flew to the Lake, by Lullaby shore
Jingo ring, a ranting Clown
Pranced from a Sky, a Moon blew down

Neath the Lake I slept in nest
A Cuckoo ! sang 'Song Cradles Best'
'Twere of a ripple dream I woke
My Lullaby Lake a 'Song Sang Spoke'

Rose from its bed of wetted place
The Lake it jumped for Clouds to make
Jigging ! Jagging ! way up high
Laughing down ere once did lie

By Lullaby Lake, where fish keep wake
Till the waters dry
They Flip with Flump, make Rain with Rump
While Blue Stars Sleep Nearby

Parody

61

SOMEONE

Someone Who Is A Friend Of Mine
Someone who is always kind
Someone who is a friend so true
Would even give their heart to you

Someone who is always there
Someone who would always share
Someone who is blessed with love
Heaven's gift from above

Someone who is so very brave
Leaves the great in the shade
Someone who is bright with smile
Lights up the dark for a while

All these words; are so so true
I Wrote This Poem; With Love For You

VALLEY VALE

Knowst I a garden
Sleepy in a vale
Where Sunlight race rave Moonbeams
Chase Long Red Rosebuds Trail

Dreamest on a Mushroom Cloud
Smiles pearly eyed a dove
Flirting down on veily greens
Mystic airs of love

Sittest in this garden
Young Robin sings with Thrush
Watching by till day is shy
Natures bloom'th blush

Skipping 'round the Garden
Rabbits bunny dance
Taunting wee the fairies
Fleeting in a trance

Knowst I a garden
Shynes glow the Primrose Pale
Nestling by, lulls Butterfly
Falls sleep the Valley Vale

FINGERPRINTS ON YOUR SOUL

I

I Left Some Fingerprints —
On Your Soul —
Some Gold — Some Silver Blue —
And When The Colours —
Tickled — Twinkled —
Became A Rainbow True

II

The Rainbow Then Began —
To Float —
Then Pattering To Your Heart
Blew Kisses Back —
To Your Soul —
"So They Could Never Part —"

III

The Rainbow Then Began —
To Smile —
The Colours —A Waltz —A Dance —
The Fingerprints —
Your Soul In Silk —
Satin Letters Of Romance —

IV

I Left Some Fingerprints —
On Your Soul —
Some Gold — Some Silver Blue —
The Rainbow Born —
A Pattering Child —

—The Pattering Child You —

SILVER SMILE

Smile a Silver Smile for me
A locket in thy face be
Be my lover my lover thee
Smile a Silver Smile on me

Snuggling warmly on my breast
Hugging hands our love caress
Keep me safe if dangers harm
Swoons my flesh; a Chain a Charm

Be We Always Pure And Chase
Mingling fondness our hearts embrace
Dream a Dreaming thought for me
Eternal lovers together we

Smile a Silver Smile for me
My Lover In A Locket Thee!

RAMBLE ROAD

RAMBLE I with you, on this fair road,
Forever will we share
Eternal, springs, of natures things, of gatherings greet there
On RAMBLE road, fall feelings flow,
Twig nests where chicks they lay
Where darkness rests, in natures crest,
Draws dawn a bright of day

On RAMBLE way, strewn stones of grey,
Plod I till weary sway
Left, Edge A Hedge, Dark Gree Its Ledge,
Brown sparrow wings away
From fonts buds grow, 'dorn flowers in grove,
Of nasal scent so sweet
Swish, swing on air, love petals rare,
Sing sounds of birdsong tweet

For what is night, but darken light, after follows day
Now leave this road, dwell dreams abode,
Comes dawn on RAMBLE way

SPRING O SPRING

The Linnet

Lingers the Linnet
To pasture abounds
Flittering ! Twittering !
Heath low:
Pastoral sounds

Sky O Lark

Sky O Lark ! Sky O Lark !
Hoover high fly the bark
Screechy thy warble
Will Spring it be dark

The Cuckoo

Cuckles young Cuckoo !
Bubbling her call
From greeny hedge bed
Come cometh the Fall

Corncrakes

And Corncrakes creak
Where Hares young rush
Fleeting in, the golden flush

74

IF EVER

If Ever I Come Back To You
It will be a "MERRY THING"
The Rain; will be of Goldust
The Winter; will be of Spring
The Sun; will "Swim" at Midnight
The Moon; will dance and Bring
The Thorns of Life; will Become
Our Youth Again A Fling

And Then When I Return To You
Let Nature do its Thing
We shall have some "TINY TOTS"
For You, To "NURSE And SING"

So Wait Till I Come Back To You
For Patience; it will Bring -
The vows "OF HONOUR"
That we Made
Will Be A "TREASURED THING"

SNOWGIRL

On Sun Drenched Hair
With Blonde Eyed Stare
I watched her with a smile
Forlone forgotten was I not
Just for a little while

A great love had enraptured me
Romance was all around
Gleaming lone and beautiful
A Snowgirl on flaked ground

My heart it beat like ne'er before
Beating from my chest
My flesh it felt so warm again
Life was at its best

She was beauty she was love
Red roses in the snow
Snow white as clouds
Where ere she went
I had longed to go

Then came the night
Fell skywards gleamly glow
Our beating hearts we had to part
The Roses and the Snow

Some day or night we'll meet again
Where I do not know
The sun drenched beauty
With Blonde Eyed Stare
Had Melted With The Snow

BRAMBLE LANE

In Bramble Lane blackberry chains, trinket all around
Romance pure maps, of pattered taps,
Embrace its raptured ground
At the end you'll see, an old oak tree,
Where love it is first born
Where lovers huddle, with kisses cuddle,
Until the dawn of morn

In Bramble Lane, are daisy chains, growing to the sky
Young lovers hold, their bodies bold, with virgin flesh so shy
For the old oak tree, old may it be, its secrets never share
A friend it is, bless will it give, 'neath its leaves of care

In Bramble Lane, there's a moonlight rain,
Moist yellows from above
Dripping, drooping gently, on the oak tree with a love
Carved in its bark, in the witnessed dark sap kisses so so quiet
Just, the rustling sounds of swishing leaves,
 Wake the deep of night

In Bramble Lane, wink stars they rain,

And make a bright of light

Rays down on flowers, in the deep dark hours,

Haunting with delight

On the old oak tree, perch birds who see,

Pondered thoughts of pairs

Who stay all night, 'til the morning sight,

Chirping beautied airs

In Bramble Lane, flower's nectar stains, on budding love of life

To mellow with glee and gracefully enjoy its love born rite

Rest dreams apart, of the oak tree dark, kindled with a smile

Ever, ever sharing, youth time, they spent a while

In Bramble Lane, romance pure reigns, time eternal lasts

Greeting lovers of long ago, return to their love pasts

For the old oak tree, is glad to see, all friends new and old

Who spent that night, in the whispered quiet,

YOUNG LOVERS KISSING BOLD

Roman Numerals

I	1	C	100
II	2	CX	110
III	3	CXI	111
IV	4	CXX	120
V	5	CC	200
V1	6	CCXX	
VII	7	220	
VIII	8	CCC	300
IX	9	CCCXX	320
X	10	CD	400
XI	11	D	500
XII	12	DC	600
XIII	13	DCC	700
XIV	14	DCCC	800
XV	15	CM	900
XVI	16	XM	990
XVII	17	M	1000
XVIII	18	MD	1500
XIX	19	MDCCC	1800
XX	20	MM	2000
XXX	30		
XL	40	MMXV	2015
L	50		
LV	55		
LX	60		
LXX	70		
LXXX	80		
LXXXVIII	88		
XC	90		

Greek Alphabet

A	α	Alpha
B	β	beta
Γ	γ	gamma
Δ	δ	delta
E	ε	epsilon
Z	ζ	zeta
H	η	eta
Θ	θ	theta
I	ι	iota
K	κ	kappa
Λ	λ	lambda
M	μ	mu
N	ν	nu
Ξ	ξ	xi
O	o	omicron
Π	π	pi
P	ρ	rho
Σ	σ	sigma
T	τ	tau
Y	υ	upsilon
Φ	φ	phi
X	ξ	chi
Ψ	Ψ	psi
Ω	ω	omega

A Bow to Beauty

I

Around the Green Hills — Nooks —
Crannies and Valleys of the lustrous,
Beautiful Wicklow Mountains of Ireland under
The "Watchful Loving Eye of Nature" and
The "Romantic Sugar Loaf Mountain" lords
The "Majestic Powerscourt Waterfall" —
Ireland's Tallest Reaching to 121m(398ft).

II

"Powerscourt Waterfall" is an "International Paradise"
And a "Proud Trophy of Nature's Beauty" —
Rambling along the "Amorous Carpet Avenue"
Pleasured by the — Pictorial Scenery
Of Beech — Oak — Larch — Pine Trees:
Born some 200 years ago, gracefully in the presence of
North California, Giant Redwoods 80m high,
And if the "Clock of Destiny" allows;
Enjoys a life of 4000 years or longer

III

An Aurous Anthology of Birds:
Chaffinch, Raven, Willow-Warbler, Cuckoo, Robins —
Harmonise the Air
With "Lute Lyrical Sounds" whilst the Trees quaver in the
Summer Sunshine, Offering Tranquil Leisures —
Sika Deer and Red Squirells prance the Meadows
— Rabbits Burrow —

IV

— Flushing "Lush" Rushing Waters —
"Rolling the Rocks — with Butterfly Bubbling — Leaps" —
Every — Tiny — Bubble Beatifying — Nature's Creation

Patrick Shortall
Author
MMXV

POWERSCOURT FALL, C° WICKLOW. 13.W.L.

83

POWERSCOURT FALL. Co. WICKLOW. 881. W.L.

POWERSCOURT FALL.

POWERSCOURT WATERFALL, C° WICKLOW 14 W.L.

POWERSCOURT FALL. CO. WICKLOW. 1663. W.L.

– Acknowledgements –

My most "Gracious Literary Thanks" to the following people
for the
Wonderful – Beautiful – Artistic
Images – Photographs
Rendering – Waterfall – Romantic
"Nestling – Amongst My Poems"

Powerscourt Waterfall

Sarah Slazenger
Aoife O'Driscoll
Carmel Byrne
Fran Byrne
Suzanne Clarke

National Library of Ireland
Gráinne Mac Lochlainn

Image credits

12, 26, 30, 32, 36, 54, 60, 74 © Carmel Byrne 2015

Back Cover, Inner Back,10, 18, 24, 34, 38, 40, 48-49, 52, 62, 64, 68, 70,
72, 76 © Fran Byrne 2015

Front Cover, Inner Front, 6, 8, 14, 16, 20, 22, 28, 48-49, 52, 62, 64, 68,
70, 72, 76 © Suzanne Clarke 2015

Images on pages 83-87 from
The Lawrence Collection
Courtesy of The National Library of Ireland.